STONEFISH

BY GOLRIZ GOLKAR

Apex is distributed by North Star Editions:
sales@northstareditions.com | 888-417-0195

Produced for Apex by Red Line Editorial.

Photographs ©: Shutterstock Images, cover, 1, 4–5, 6, 7, 8–9, 10–11, 12, 14, 15, 16–17, 18–19, 22–23, 24, 26–27, 27, 29; Georgette Douwma/Nature Picture Library/Alamy, 20–21

Library of Congress Control Number: 2022901418

ISBN
978-1-63738-287-5 (hardcover)
978-1-63738-323-0 (paperback)
978-1-63738-394-0 (ebook pdf)
978-1-63738-359-9 (hosted ebook)

Printed in the United States of America
Mankato, MN
082022

NOTE TO PARENTS AND EDUCATORS

Apex books are designed to build literacy skills in striving readers. Exciting, high-interest content attracts and holds readers' attention. The text is carefully leveled to allow students to achieve success quickly. Additional features, such as bolded glossary words for difficult terms, help build comprehension.

TABLE OF CONTENTS

CHAPTER 1

HUNTING AND HIDING

A stonefish rests on the seafloor. Its body blends in with the rocks around it. The stonefish spots a shrimp nearby. It grabs the shrimp in its big mouth.

Stonefish live in shallow ocean waters.

A tiger shark tries to eat the stonefish. But the fish has spines on its back. They sting the shark. It swims away in pain.

Tiger sharks are one of the few animals that hunt stonefish.

Stonefish tend to hide among rocks on the seafloor.

The stonefish hides again. It waits for more prey to swim by.

Stonefish may hold still and wait on the seafloor for hours at a time.

BLENDING IN

Stonefish have thick, bumpy skin. Sometimes, plants grow on their bodies. The bumps and plants help stonefish hide on the seafloor. The fish look like rocks or corals.

CHAPTER 2

HiDDEN CREATURES

There are five different types of stonefish. Most grow about 16 inches (41 cm) long. All have wide bodies and flat fins.

Some stonefish are bright colors. Others are mainly gray.

Stonefish are often gray or brown. They may have red, yellow, or orange spots. These colors help stonefish blend in with their surroundings.

SLOW SWIMMERS

Stonefish cannot swim very fast. They don't chase prey. Instead, they hide and wait for prey to come to them. They also hide to stay safe from predators.

The horrid stonefish is one type of stonefish. It blends in with weeds, stones, and sand.

The fin on a stonefish's back has 12 to 14 sharp spines. Each spine has a sac filled with poison. The poison can hurt or kill predators.

A stonefish's spines are long and sharp, like needles.

Some stonefish are tan. This color helps them blend in with sand.

CHAPTER 3

LiFE IN THE OCEAN

Stonefish live in the Indian and Pacific Oceans. They often rest on coral reefs. They also live in bays or muddy areas.

The reef stonefish lives near Australia's Great Barrier Reef.

Stonefish mainly eat shrimp and small fish. They snatch prey with their mouths and swallow the prey whole.

FAST FACT

Stonefish can survive out of water for up to 24 hours. They take in **oxygen** through their skin.

Stonefish can open their large mouths and suck prey inside.

Stonefish live alone except for when they mate. After mating, females lay eggs on the seafloor. Young fish hatch from the eggs.

Stonefish mate once a year.

LOTS OF EGGS

A female stonefish can lay up to one million eggs at a time. But not all the babies become adults. Other fish often eat them. Having lots of eggs helps stonefish survive.

CHAPTER 4

DANGEROUS FISH

Stonefish don't use their poison on prey. Instead, it defends them from predators. These predators include stingrays, sharks, and sea snakes.

Stonefish can use their fins to dig and bury themselves in sand. This helps them hide.

A stonefish's spines pop up when a predator touches it. The sacs in the spines release poison. The predator gets a painful sting.

FAST FACT

Sea snakes sometimes eat stonefish. They kill the fish with a poisonous bite.

 Sea snakes dive to search for food in coral reefs.

⚠ WARNING

STONEFISH IN THIS AREA

Signs at some beaches warn swimmers to watch out for stonefish.

HIDDEN WEAPONS

Stonefish have hidden spines inside their cheeks. When a stonefish is threatened, these spines pop out like knives. The spines glow, too. The fish uses them to scare predators.

People sometimes step on stonefish by accident. They can be hurt badly. However, heat and medicine can weaken the poison. They help people heal.

Stonefish stings cause bad pain and sickness. They must be treated right away.

COMPREHENSION QUESTIONS

Write your answers on a separate piece of paper

1. Write a few sentences describing how stonefish catch food.

2. Do you think running away or hiding is usually a better way to escape danger? Why?

3. Which body part releases a stonefish's poison?

　　A. its teeth

　　B. its skin

　　C. its spines

4. Why would having lots of eggs help stonefish survive?

　　A. More eggs means more babies will survive to become adults.

　　B. When stonefish lay eggs, they get stronger.

　　C. Stonefish mothers eat their eggs.

5. What does release mean in this book?

The sacs in the spines release poison.
The predator gets a painful sting.

  A. to take in
  B. to send out
  C. to float

6. What does defends mean in this book?

Stonefish don't use their poison on prey.
Instead, it defends them from predators.

  A. keeps quiet
  B. makes bigger
  C. keeps safe

Answer key on page 32.

GLOSSARY

bays
Bodies of water partly surrounded by land that empty into larger bodies of water such as oceans.

corals
Tiny animals that look similar to plants. Large numbers of corals grow together to form reefs.

mate
To form a pair and come together to have babies.

oxygen
A type of gas that animals need to breathe to survive.

predators
Animals that hunt and eat other animals.

prey
Animals that are hunted and eaten by other animals.

sac
A pouch in an animal or plant that holds air or liquid.

spines
Sharp and pointy parts of animals or plants.

TO LEARN MORE

BOOKS

Buckley, James, Jr. *Needles of Pain! Stonefish Attack.* Minneapolis: Bearport Publishing, 2021.

Harvey, Derek. *Nature's Deadliest Creatures*. London: DK Children, 2018.

Hyde, Natalie. *Animal Disguises*. New York: Crabtree Publishing, 2020.

ONLINE RESOURCES

Visit www.apexeditions.com to find links and resources related to this title.

ABOUT THE AUTHOR

Golriz Golkar is a former elementary school teacher. She has written more than 50 nonfiction books for children. She loves to sing and spend time with her young daughter.

INDEX

ANSWER KEY:
1. Answers will vary; 2. Answers will vary; 3. C; 4. A; 5. B; 6. C